Setting the Pace

Peak performance for young and beginning runners

by

Sue E. Jones

Setting the Pace

Library of Congress Control Number
2013900672

ISBN-13: 978-1481908993
ISBN-10: 1481908995

Front cover: *Runnin' with the Wolves* finish line
Photo by Hannah Frazier

Acknowledgments

I would like to thank my Lord, Jesus Christ, for saving me and putting the desire to run, coach, and write this book into my heart. I want to thank my loving husband of over 32 years, Alan, who has encouraged me and, in many instances, facilitated my running and coaching. He is the love of my life and my best friend. I want to thank my four children: Becky, Beth, Mark, and Micah for patiently waiting many long hours at the finish lines of the numerous races while I ran. They are my joy and delight and prompted me to start a homeschool cross country team. I want to especially thank Micah for jump-starting me to write this book and always making me laugh.

I want to thank my sister, Paula, for her patience and help with the editing of this book and for being the best friend I could ask for. I want to thank all of the runners who have ever been on the Peaks View Pacers for allowing me the honor of coaching them and watching them grow into godly young men and women. And finally, I want to thank Jerome Loy and Barbara Lucy for breathing life into our new team and allowing us to compete. Jerome planted the actual idea of cross country running into my mind by inviting us to his *Runnin' with the Wolves Cross Country Invitational* and it was Barbara who invited us to all of her home meets and gave us our first preliminary cross country schedule. May God bless you all!

Dedication

"Commit to the Lord whatever you do, and your plans will succeed."

Prov.16:3 (NIV)

Table of Contents

Preface...i

Introduction...iv

Chapter 1: Who am I? 1

Chapter 2: Less is Best 3

Chapter 3: Beginnings- Story of a New Runner 9

Chapter 4: Phases of a Training Plan 15

Chapter 5: Run Safe 25

Chapter 6: Creating a Weekly Training Schedule..29

Chapter 7: Cold Weather Running 37

Chapter 8: Nutrition 41

Chapter 9: Stretching 51

Chapter 10: All in a Day 57

Chapter 11: The Race 61

Chapter 12: This and That 73

Appendix A: Sample Training Plans 83

Appendix B: Sample Workouts 87

References:...93

Setting the Pace

Preface

As I was preparing to run the Boston marathon, I was introduced to a new type of running: trail running. This type of running was supposed to be easier on a person's joints than road running, with the added bonus of beautiful scenery to view along the way. In Lynchburg, Virginia, we were fortunate to have a new rails-to-trails bike path and trail system in place. With this, we were able to take advantage of several trails during our lunch time runs. It was on one such run that I twisted my ankle pretty badly. I was able to finish the run but my ankle would continue to swell after each run for the next three months. I had an x-ray taken of it and was told that I had a hairline fracture in my ankle bone and that I should use a brace for any more training. I was very blessed to have a doctor who was almost as determined to see me run Boston as I was myself. So, with this bulky brace stuffed into my running shoe, I continued to train.

Finally, I was there, walking around the staging area in Hopkinton, Massachusetts, with a brace clear up to my knee waiting for the start time of the 2000 Boston Marathon. With the call to the line given, I put my brace in my pack to await me at the finish line and prayed I would be able to run without any problems. What an experience. What a crowd.

What a very cold day to run a marathon. The wind was very strong and the sun very shy in peaking out to warm us up. I ran with long sleeves, headband and gloves the whole way and at one point I took off my headband to wrap around my poor numb, Gatorade drenched hand to try to keep it from freezing. The crowds were amazing. The cheers passing Wellesley College were as loud as they say they are. I remember crying on and off for the last six miles as I marveled at the shoulder-to-shoulder crowd standing five deep just to see me, so it seemed. It was a very humbling experience and my emotions were intensified by my poor physical response to the elements and terrain. When I crossed the finish line, I was so happy to have been given the honor of running in the Boston Marathon!

Back at the hotel, soaking in an ice bath, a knock came at the door. Could it be flowers for me? No, my husband and children had sent me something much better. They had followed my progress on the website and had printed out my split times (times given every few miles) along with the unofficial results and faxed them to my hotel room with drawings from each of my children with their own interpretation of mommy's race in Boston that day. How special that whole experience was to me.

It would be an understatement to say that running has been a major part of my life. I have shaped my choices, my career, and my family around running. It is more than a hobby to me; it is a lifestyle. I have found immense joy in running and wanted to communicate this great love to a younger generation; that is why I began coaching cross country teams.

For those who don't know, cross country is running, except without all the stipulations and guidelines one would find on a track. It's dirty, sometimes bloody and sweaty, and altogether some of the most fun a person could ever have in his running career.

I started coaching middle school and high school students almost by chance. It's complicated to say exactly how the events that led up to me creating the first homeschool cross country team fell into place. Whether it was divine intervention or not, I found myself in a place where I was translating my love of running to young athletes who were eager and ready. I cannot emphasize enough how much this meant to me and still means to me; it makes me feel as if I have been a part of something way beyond myself. There I was, running beside my own children and other kids their age. Since my initial days as a cross country coach, I have earned several certifications as a running coach, and I have been the vice-president of a local running group that oversees our area's road races.

It all boils down to running. Running is what I love. Running is who I am.

Introduction

The thing that inspired me the most to write this book was the Peaks View Pacers. The Peaks View Pacers is a homeschool cross country team that I helped found in 2001. I was head coach and administrator for the next 10 years and, over the course of that time, I tried using the popular training models with my runners. This was a frustration to me, as my runners were unable to handle the amount of miles these training models recommended or the intensities that they suggested. Thankfully, I am a "fixer" by nature and am married to an engineer, so these two things partnered together and I quickly began to customize these programs. Each year seemed to show me something new that I could or could not use with my runners. When questioned by my team on various topics in the past few years, I found myself saying, "I should write a book." That is when I began writing down our workouts, the intensity and amount of miles, along with notes about each. The more I wrote, the more I realized I really needed to get this information into the hands of runners. I hope this book will do that.

I address the majority of this book as if I were speaking directly to a group of runners. While my initial goal was to write a book specifically for the young runner, I have found many of these principles to be of value to the beginning runner of any age, as well.

 Chapter One

Who am I?

I was born in upstate New York. The youngest of six children with a nurse for a mother and a doctor for a father, it is no wonder that health would eventually become a big part of my life. Even though both of my parents were in the medical field, my family has been touched with major health issues. My father died at 65 as a result of complications from diabetes, my brother had a heart attack before the age of 50, and three of us children have hypothyroidism. Though the stage was set for me to be careful with my health, it took awhile for me to fully embrace it.

My parents divorced when I was seven; as a result, my weight took a beating. It seemed to me that my parents competed for my affection with goodies and treats. I can remember sitting at home with my sister in front of the television set with nothing but cookies and milk, dunking and eating, dunking and eating. At Dad's there were always chips and dip. By the time I was in the sixth grade I weighed 150 pounds. My eyes were squished up into slits because my cheeks were so chubby. My mother noticed my sister's and my weight gain and offered us a way out. She offered to pay us a dollar for every pound we lost and we would have to pay her a dollar for every pound we gained over the summer. We each lost twenty pounds and then the summer ended and the money deal was off. Before I knew it I was back up to almost 150 lbs.

When I was fifteen, my mother and I moved to Virginia and there was a long walk to the bus stop, almost a full mile. I walked the mile each way every day and soon I was losing weight. The walk and resultant weight loss made me interested in exercise and nutrition in general.

Watching my weight and trying to make wise food choices have become a way of life for me. But it wasn't until later, when I was in college, that I began running. Running soon became such a part of my life that I identify myself in every way as a runner. What first started off as a way to lose and maintain my weight became so much more. Now I hope to help others experience the joy I get when I run.

 Chapter Two

Less is Best

Over the years as a middle school and high school cross country coach, I have seen many runners put in too many miles and do too many hard workouts and end up injured. Year after year it seemed to be the same. Those runners who were running fifty miles a week or more would spend the end of the season on the sidelines injured. There are many books and articles on the market that discuss training plans and running cycles, but they all seem geared toward adults. I began adjusting these training plans to better fit my runners.

 My personal running style has evolved into a rather simple statement: "Less is best." My experience has proven that runners remain uninjured when running a modest amount of miles while still achieving their goals.

One time, I was approached by a dad to coach his daughter in some post-season races. I had seen her at some of the middle school meets and knew she was a good runner. She was in the 6th grade and playing on a volleyball team, but had really shown some promise in cross country. When we first met, I asked how many miles she was currently running each week. I was shocked to hear that she was only running in the meets, which put her total weekly miles at around 4 miles. With only one month to get her ready for the back-to-back weekend races, I had to keep in mind this low mileage when planning her training schedule. Therefore, I added two more days of running to her weekly schedule, for a total of 10 miles. Even with such low weekly mileage, she finished 6th in the USA Track & Field Junior Olympics and 2nd place at Footlocker Cross Country South Regional Championships for her age group.

Another year, I was asked to coach a young man in the 8th grade for a post-season meet. He wanted to run the same Footlocker Cross Country South Regional Championships in Charlotte, NC, in late November. He had run the 3k (1.89 mile) race the year before and had finished 31st, just out of the medals. Finishing a season in which he won every race he had entered, he was hoping to do the same in Charlotte as well. I encouraged him to reset his goals to bettering last year's time and getting a medal. These seemed more realistic. After setting up a weekly workout schedule, I quickly learned that he was going through a growing phase and that his knees were hurting every other day. He had to take more rest and easy days than we had first planned in order for his knees to recover from the weekly speed and hill work. He kept a record of his weekly mileage and over a five week period he rarely ran more than 20 miles each week. Nevertheless, he entered the race well prepared and ended up taking 43 seconds off his last year's time and he finished 5th in his age group. The following week he ran a road race 5k and set a new personal best time for that distance by almost a minute.

These are two fine examples of how low mileage can still produce good results.

Let's take a more in-depth look at the philosophy of "less is best" as it pertains to training and young runners. It is important to take into consideration the fact that their young bodies are growing and developing. Young people ages 11-18 are going through puberty with all its physical demands and it is of the utmost importance that they get plenty of rest and the proper nutrition. When the demands of a running program are added, it can be a recipe for disaster. But it doesn't have to be. If you use caution when planning, you can develop a training plan that allows you to safely train and compete while avoiding injury.

Recommendations for these age groups are that middle school runners run 15 miles or less and high school runners run between 20 and 30 miles each week.

Breaking this down even more, runners who are 10 years old and younger should run no more than 10 miles per week and those who are 11-13 years should keep their weekly mileage to a maximum of 15 miles. Runners in these two age groups should run no farther than 5 miles at one time. Runners 14 and older should run somewhere between 20-30 miles per week with a maximum long run of 10 miles. As some youths develop earlier than others, size and development must be taken into account when determining exactly when the young runner is ready to increase his weekly mileage.

I have allowed a few of my older high school runners to run up to 40 miles per week, but I strongly discourage running any more than that. I really believe that running farther than 40 miles per week at this age will do more harm than good.

Two other mottos I like to use with my runners are, "Quality is better than quantity," and "Live to run another day." When keeping the total number of miles per week down, it is very important to make each mile count. This is the quality aspect of training. Don't run junk miles. Even if you are out for an easy run, that easy run is on your schedule for a purpose: to aid recovery from the previous day's hard workout while increasing overall endurance. This will allow you to have energy to be involved in other activities as well as to have you ready for the next hard workout.

 Hoping to foster a love for running and an appreciation for being physically fit, I tell runners that the ultimate goal is to "live to run another day." This idea can take off much of the stress of running and the pressure to perform. If the young person runs too much or gets injured too often, he may become discouraged. Too often I see star high school athletes who finish school and never want to run again. This is a shame because studies show the health benefits of continuing to be active your whole life (Healthfinder, 2012). And running is an excellent form of this type of physical activity.

At the end of each cross country season, I would hold a banquet for my runners. This was my way of congratulating them and letting the spotlight shine on each one. My husband would put together a DVD of photos that highlighted the season, complete with music and narration, and I would hand out awards. I also made it a point to get a guest speaker to come and speak to them. One year

I had an athlete speak who would later go on to win the NCAA Cross Country Championships. He was so inspiring, but even among his peers, he was unusual in the amount of miles he was able to run each week. While I applauded him and his accomplishments, I needed to remind my runners that there is a big difference between a 15-year-old runner and a 22-year-old runner, physiologically speaking. It is important to keep the motivated young runner from putting in too many miles too early in his running career.

As a post script, I have wondered if this type of training didn't have a negative effect on the NCAA champ, as I have not heard anything more of him since that race (Latter, 2011).

Resist the urge to follow the crowd by running too many miles.

You may ask, "Is running at an early age beneficial at all?" Yes. Research has shown that runners, particularly young women, who start running before the age of 20 and continue with this weight bearing exercise into their adult years, greatly reduce their risk of getting osteoporosis as an older person (Hind & Burrows, 2007). What a great way to protect yourself from a debilitating disease, by running now.

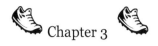 Chapter 3

Beginnings:
Story of a New Runner

While I was still in high school, my mother had a long drive to and from work and she would often comment about all the people she saw out running. I never really thought about it at the time, but that comment would later come back to me as words of inspiration. At that time, the Virginia Ten Miler was becoming one of the top 10 road races in the country. It was probably some of the people training for this race that she saw while driving.

Sometime later, I was living with my sister while going to college and our refrigerator held little more than a head of lettuce and our cupboard only some saltine crackers. It was at this time that I met my future husband. His mother was a true southern chef and soon I was eating meal after meal of her fine cooking. As I have said, I never had an aversion to eating, so I was fitting right in. However, all those tasty meals began to add up.

I can recall the first time I ever considered running. My future husband and I were at an all-you-can eat buffet and I was going back for seconds. "Are you sure you want seconds?" he asked politely. "Why?" I asked, not seeing the meaning of his question. "Well," he said, "my mother says your thighs are getting fat."

After getting over the initial shock of that statement, I remembered my mother's stories of all the runners in town and I knew what I had to do. Start running. And run I did. And I still ended up marrying him.

Federal officials say Americans need 60 minutes a day of moderate activity to control weight, plus a diet that emphasizes whole grains, fruits, and vegetables (Fiore, 2010). A good running program can help accomplish this.

My first running experience still remains a very vivid one for me. I went to our local K-Mart and bought a pair of "tennis shoes." Mind you, this was 1979 and there were no real running specific shoes to be found at K-Mart. Nevertheless, the next morning I got up early, pulled on a pair of denim jeans and a long-sleeved flannel shirt, laced up my new shoes, and headed out the door. I should mention that, at the time, I was smoking close to two packs of cigarettes a day. I barely made it to the mailbox before collapsing, wheezing and coughing. The first thing I had to do was to shelve the cigarettes. After that, it took nearly a whole month before I could run a full mile without stopping. I stuck with it and soon the next mile was a little easier to do. It seemed like before I knew it I was running farther and farther.

Meanwhile, the "tennis shoes" I had been running in were as stiff as a board and soon my arches started to hurt; I felt as though I was becoming flat-footed and my shoes began to fall apart. I knew I needed to have help from someone who knew something about running and shoes. I went to Straub's Specialty Sports, a running store in our city. I was fitted and sized for shoes and things that I didn't even know happened in a shoe store. They looked at the bottom of the shoes I had been running in and found that I had completely worn the whole outside corners of the bottoms off. I didn't even know that I was supposed to look at the bottom of my shoes. And so, I bought my first pair of true running shoes and I've gotten fitted and sized for shoes ever since.

I later learned that Rudy Straub, the owner of Straub's Specialty Sports, was the founder of the Virginia Ten Miler, the race that prompted the runners who my mother saw as she drove back and forth into work. I remembered my mother's comment about those runners when I started my own cycle of running. It's amazing how God brought together all these events to form my early running history.

11

My first race

I was still attending the local community college when I started running with my biology lab partner. She told me about a race to raise money for world hunger or another charity and suggested that we run it. It was a 10k, which I found out was 6.2 miles long, and she assured me we could finish it. At the time, we were only running 4 miles twice a week, but she promised me that "a person can run 3 times as far as her training without dying." Very reassuring!

On race day, we started at the very back of the pack with no illusions of grandeur. The race started at Jefferson Forest High School and wound its way up and down the hills into Ivy Lake and back. With about one mile left to go, I could tell my running partner was anxious to keep running while I was feeling the effects of the warm weather and the heat from the sun, so I told her to go on ahead. Not long after she left me, I saw the sag car, the car that comes behind the last person to make sure they make it in. This car pulled up next to me and the people in it asked if I minded them going on. Sure, I said, wondering who would eventually find my body. When I finally made my way to the finish, I noticed people getting into their cars to drive home. They were polite and cheered for me, but the salt that granulated on my face and the dry heaves that were to come did not put me in a positive frame of mind. I told my husband that I would "never run another race again!"

I have now learned to never say, "Never." They say, "Time heals all wounds." And today, more than 180 races later, I can look back on the irony of my remark about that first race and laugh.

 Chapter 4

Phases of a Training Plan

 It is important to be conservative in your approach to training. Adding too many miles too soon can lead to injury, so be sure to add miles slowly.

Developing a training plan doesn't need to be difficult. In many ways it is like a puzzle. Once you look at the whole picture, placing each individual piece in its proper place becomes easy. The first things to consider are the pieces to your puzzle, such as how many days a week you have that you can devote to running and how many weeks away from your goal race you are. The second is to understand each of the phases of your training. And the final thing is to put these pieces into place on your calendar. After you do all these things you are ready to begin.

I like Arthur Lydiard's "backward" method of setting up a training plan (Lydiard, 2004). Simply put, it has you select your goal race and count the weeks backward to the current date. I try to sit down with a calendar at the beginning of each year, or season, and mark off the key race, or races, in which I want to run well. Then I choose a major goal race and count back the number of weeks until I get to where I am currently on the calendar. I want to make sure I have twelve weeks or more until the main goal race.

Why twelve weeks? Most training plans use twelve as the number of weeks needed to take a runner all the way through training and deposit him on the starting line ready for that race. This is why starting to run in early June or before is very important in preparing for the cross country season that begins in early September.

There are six phases of training and they are: base, strength, speed, taper, race, and recovery.

I have modified the Road Runners Club of America (RRCA) model of training cycles for young runners

16

by breaking down the sharpening cycle into two separate phases: strength and speed (RRCA, 2009). This helps the young runner better understand exactly what he is working on in training so that he can more accurately focus on the goal of each specific phase.

The **base phase** is the period of time when you build up your weekly mileage to a point where you can safely handle harder workouts. This phase can last from 4-12 weeks or even longer.

It is important to know how many weekly miles you need to reach before adding those harder workouts. As was recommended in the earlier chapter, runners 10 years old and younger should keep their mileage to a maximum of 10 miles per week. Runners 11-13 years of age should run a total of 10-15 miles a week. Runners 14 years and older should run somewhere between 20-30 miles each week, with an absolute maximum of 40 miles. Every runner is different and a constant assessment of your physical well-being is always in order. Now that you have your total weekly mileage in mind, how can you get there?

💡 The 10% rule is a good guideline to safely add miles each week. This rule states that you should only add 10% of your weekly mileage to the next week's mileage.

For example, if a runner is just starting back from taking the winter off, and he runs 10 miles the first week. The next week he runs 11 miles and then 12 the next until he builds up to 20 miles. After that, he can add 2 miles for the next week. Adding no more than 10% of one's weekly miles ensures that the base mileage is built gradually and without injury.

If you are a beginning runner, you can start off by run/walking 1 mile every other day until you can run a whole mile without stopping to walk. Then add one additional day each week until you are running 5 days a week. (See Appendix A for more in-depth training plans.)

💡 It is a good idea to run a little farther in training than the actual race distance. If you race 2 miles, a run of 3 miles will help build your confidence for race day and ultimately you will run faster.

The **strength phase** piece to your puzzle can last from 4-8 weeks and will include hill repeats, running drills, and preliminary speed workouts that will include pick-ups, and fartleks.

Hill repeats are short runs of up to one minute in duration run up a fairly decent hill. They are intended to build muscle strength and begin introducing some speed into the workouts.

Running drills can be added to the middle or the end of a run to target specific muscles in order to strengthen them. Examples of these are high knees, butt-kicks, skipping, criss-cross sideways running, and strides. Drills can help your overall running form while strengthening specific muscles. (See Appendix B for a description of each.)

Pick-ups are short, quick runs, usually 30 seconds to 1 minute in length, with the same amount of speed time as recovery time. These are run a little slower than race pace, with running form as the focus. Pickups begin to introduce speed into the training plan.

Fartleks are not only a fun word to say, but also a great way to add short bursts of speed to your workout. Meaning "speed play" in Swedish, a fartlek is running hard for a short distance, for example from one mailbox to the next or one utility pole to the next and then returning to your normal pace. Fartleks can add a fun dimension to your workout. Fartleks differ from pick-ups in that speed is the focus in the fartlek.

The **speed phase** lasts from 4-8 weeks and adds faster timed sessions to your training. This is the time to hit the track or other measured path for some timed intervals. For cross country runners 400 meter repeats is your bread and butter. If you never get to run any other distance, running 400 meter repeats will be enough to improve speed and lower times. Therefore, it is always good to begin with them. When determining how many repeats to run, go back to the 10% rule.

In this instance, the 10% rule means to run only 10% of your weekly mileage in actual speed.

An example of this is the young athlete who has built her mileage up to 20-25 miles per week. She can then run 10% of that, or 2-2.5 miles of speed, in her track sessions. This could be a session that consists of 8-10 x 400 meter repeats.

For an explanation of what this would look like, keep in mind that 400 meters equals one lap on most outdoor tracks. After warming up with .5-1 mile of easy jogging, the runner would run hard for one lap and then jog easy for the second lap. Using this example, she would then do that 8 to 10 times, finishing with a cool down of .5 -1 mile of easy jogging. Since she has 4-8 weeks to work on speed, I recommend, as in every aspect of training the young athlete, that she start off easy and build gradually.

This would mean her first track workout would be 4-6 x 400 meters. The range is given to see how well she has developed a sense of pacing and endurance and strength from the previous two phases. If she continued to run each 400 meters in about the same time, she could continue up to 6 repeats the first week. But, if after a few repeats, her time began to slow by 3 or more seconds, she would not do another repeat, but run her cool down; her speed session would be over.

The next week she would try to add more 400's to her workout, maintaining her pace. As time in the training plan allows, other distances can be integrated into the track sessions.

💡 If you can't make it to the track, substitute a tempo run for the speed work session.

Tempo runs are runs of 1-2 miles, or 15-20 minutes, that are run a little slower than 10k race pace, or at a "comfortably hard" pace (Luff, 2011). They are designed to improve endurance and speed by raising your anaerobic threshold, that is, the point in your body where lactic acid begins to build up (Luff, 2012). Tempo runs always include a warm up and cool down of anywhere from .5 mile to 2 miles in length, with the tempo part in the middle.

The last three phases are the **taper**, **race**, and **recovery phases;** these will overlap and be repeated several times throughout the cross country season.

The **taper** is when you cut your mileage back or take time off completely in preparation for a race. This is a short phase, the length of which is determined based on the distance of the upcoming race. The middle school runner will race distances of 2 miles or less and the high school runner will race a 5k, or 3.1 mile, distance. Since these are both relatively short races, the taper will last only a day or two at most. Therefore, the runner can reduce his mileage on the day leading up to the race, or take it completely off, as his taper.

The **race phase** is the actual race and lasts only one day. The race will be repeated several times during the season leading up to the "goal race" which will conclude the racing season.

The **recovery phase** can last from one day to up to twelve weeks. During the cross country season, the recovery will be the first day or two following each meet. These days will need to be incorporated into the training plan. At the end of the season a longer recovery period should be scheduled.

The longer recovery phase at the end of the season is a time when the runner may take up to three months off completely. This is the time when the body can rebuild and recover from the hard training of the past few months. Look at this as a reward for all the hard work you did during the season and allow your body time to heal.

Recovery is every bit as important as any of the other phases. This is a great time to do some cross training by adding swimming, biking, or other activities that were set aside during the cross country season. Just as the earth was created in six days and on the seventh day God rested, so the young athlete must take time off from running for a prolonged rest for her body to recover.

Now that you understanding each of these phases, or pieces to the puzzle, you can place them on the calendar and watch your training plan take shape. You will want to be sure you include all of the phases: base, strength, speed, taper, race, and recovery as you plan. Starting with the goal race and working backward, place your race and taper days onto your calendar, usually only one day of taper for each meet. Continue working back through the calendar and see how many weeks can be devoted to the speed phase. Then place the strength phase weeks and finally, add the base phase weeks onto your calendar. The base phase will be the longest and is where you start your training.

Placing the training phase "pieces" of the puzzle onto your calendar will help develop the whole picture of your training schedule. You will then be ready to piece together the next training puzzle: the weekly training schedule.

 Chapter 5

Run Safe

Good to my word, I did not run another race for three years following that first 10k. However, I did continue to run. I loved running! I felt so free and in tune with nature and God when I was running. It wasn't long before I was running 5 miles each time out.

I had earned my Associates Degree at Central Virginia Community College and was ready to move to Tennessee to go to Tennessee Tech University to get my Bachelor's Degree. With less than a month before we moved, I was out on one of these glorious runs when I noticed something out of the ordinary. Big dump trucks were driving on my secluded gravel road. Truck after truck passed by me kicking up dust when suddenly a truck drove in the opposite direction. This truck drove in the same direction that I was running. As a woman running alone, I was always paying attention and this was no exception. My normal run had me run out and back and then take a short walk break along this gravel section. I recalled a side "Lover's Lane" turn-off along that section and wondered, half-seriously, if this dump truck had gone down there. I kept running, thinking that I would just get past that section and see that my mind was playing tricks with me and that there was no truck there and then I could take my walk break. I was also praying.

As I thought all this, I began picking up my pace, reasoning that the faster I got past the point where the truck might have turned off, the sooner I would pass any potential danger and be done with my suspicions. As I neared the turn off and looked, there was the truck. Both doors and the hood were open but no one was in sight. I was glad I had picked up my pace and I continued cruising along quickly, thinking that all was well, when I heard a shout. I turned around to see a short, rotund man in the middle of the road running after me!

At this point, all I remember is hearing gravel spin as I turned and sprinted faster than I ever had in my life. Time seemed to stand still and in too short a time my legs began to feel like I was wearing cement shoes. I knew I could not keep running this fast. When I rounded the next turn in the road I dared to look back and saw an empty road behind me.

Thankfully, I was only a short distance from my house and I made it home safely. Needless to say, this shook me up and upset me greatly. I was frustrated because this person had taken away the peaceful safety I had felt when I ran that beautiful back road. I did not run again for several months and at first only around a track and with a running partner. I have since learned some safety measures for running and I have not had another encounter with a potential predator since. Praise God!

Safety tips for running alone or with a group

1. Always be aware of your surroundings.
2. Try to find other runners in your area to run with.
3. If you must run alone, carry a stick or pepper spray, if at all possible.
4. Run facing traffic and wear brightly colored clothes.
5. Run during the day or in well-lit areas.
6. If you must run at dawn or dusk, wear a flashing light and reflective vest.
7. If a car approaches you, stay far enough away that you are not in arms reach. Memorize the license plates.
8. Always look strangers in the eye; it gives the appearance of confidence. You are less likely to become a victim if you appear confident.
9. Vehicles always have the right of way. Be cautious.

I spent two years at Tennessee Tech University getting my Bachelor's Degree in Elementary Education. During my final year, my new running partner asked me to run a 10k race with her. We had been running 5 miles or more on most days and I felt in great shape. I knew I could finish and not feel as awful as I had in my first race. We agreed to run together the whole way and, in this race, it was my turn to be the encourager. My friend was having a tough time and I spent much of the last two miles talking to her about the nice cool breeze, the refreshments they would have for us when we finished, and anything but the actual race. The last miles were very long, but we finally made it to the finish. As we were enjoying the post-race foods and drinks, we watched the awards ceremony. While laughing and talking, I noticed a girl from one of my classes go up onto the stage to receive an award. The competitive seed in me began to grow. If she could get a medal, I wondered if I could.

Five months later, after determining to run faster in the next race, I was the one going onto the stage to receive my first award: a duffle bag with the race logo on it for placing in my age group. I had taken 16 minutes off my 10k time. "Hmm," I thought. "I wonder if I actually *trained* what would happen?" And so my training began.

 Chapter 6

Creating a Weekly Training Schedule

"Hard work beats Talent when Talent won't work hard." – Kevin Durant

Now that you have your calendar pieced together with the phases of training, you are ready for your next training puzzle: the weekly training schedule. Just like the phases are important to your overall training plan, there are three main days in your training week that need to be given special consideration. These three days are the hard days of your week in which you increase the intensity of your run by, at first, increasing your miles and, later, by adding more strenuous workouts.

It is very important to treat the hard days of your week with special consideration because they add additional stress to your body. Therefore, you want to follow each hard day with an easy day. Easy days are days in which you run at a pace that is comfortable enough for you to carry on a conversation while running. Easy days can also be days when you cross train by biking, hiking, or

29

swimming instead of running. Please keep in mind that cross training, when used for an easy day, needs to be taken easy. Don't push yourself hard in these other activities. You can also take a day off completely from exercising. This easy day is called a rest day.

As mentioned above, there are three hard days each week. In the base phase of your training, these three days are gradual increases in mileage. In the strength phase hard days will consist of speed, hills, and a long run. Your speed days will consist of pick-ups and fartleks. When you move into the speed phase, you will continue with your hard days being speed, hills, and a long run, but your speed days will be more structured, running intervals on the track or other measured path.

In both the strength and speed phases, your hill days are days when you build strength by running hills or doing drills and they will remain pretty constant throughout these two phases. Hill days can be removed all together if you find your body needs more rest, by replacing them with easy days. In each of the three mentioned phases, the long run is exactly that, a run that is about twice as long as a normal easy day's run.

💡 Even though the long run is technically a hard day in your training week, it should be run at a "conversational pace" or a pace easy enough that you can carry on a conversation with someone. The fact that it is almost twice as long as your normal run is what makes it a hard day.

💡 Hard Days should not occur on back-to-back days of the week.

Remember how you pieced together your training plan using Lydiard's backward approach? Your weekly schedule can be assembled in much the same way. Begin by place the long run into your week, making sure you allow enough time in your day to complete it. Long runs can last up to an hour for some high school runners. Most training plans place the long run on a weekend day, but the high school and middle school athlete can be more flexible and can choose a different day of the week.

Looking at your week now that the long run is in place, you want to work backward. Remembering the tip of no hard runs back-to-back, you will add an easy day, then a hard, and so on ending with two easy days together. Your completed puzzle finally looks like this: Easy, Easy, Hard, Easy, Hard, Easy, and Hard, with the last hard day being the long run (RRCA, 2009).

Remember, the long run does not have to be Saturday. Keeping this weekly pattern, you can place your days according to your availability to train.

💡 The long run is the most important piece of the puzzle and, because of the longer time on your feet, requires two days of recovery.

💡 The long run can be replaced by the race day once the racing season starts.

After the easy and hard days are in place, you can begin to see what the picture of your training week will look like. Remembering the training phases of base, strength, speed, taper, race, and recovery will help you in your actual training schedule.

If you are in the base phase, you are building your mileage up. The three hard days each week will be increases in miles with the third hard day being an even longer run of almost twice the distance of an easy day. This day is known as the long run. (See the 10% rule for more guidelines in mileage building and see Appendix A for sample training plans.)

If you are in the strength building phase, the first two hard days of the week will be drills and hill work and the third hard day will be the long run. Just before the speed phase, begin alternating drills with pick-ups and fartleks. This begins to introduce speed and gives the runner a feel for faster running.

If you are in the speed training phase, the first hard day will be a track session or tempo run, followed by hill runs on the second hard day. (See Appendix B for sample speed sessions and hill workouts.) The third hard day is reserved for the long run and will be switched out for meets once the season starts.

Remember that the taper, race, and recovery phases will overlap during the season. Therefore, the taper will be the day before each meet. The meet is the race, and the recovery is the day or two following each meet.

Once the goal race has been run, medals awarded, and the season is over, be sure to take time off from running to allow your body time to heal from the hard training.

When the racing season has one or more races each week, the middle and high school runner must juggle the taper, race, and recovery while keeping his base and speed.

This is tricky, but not impossible. In a seven day period, here is an example of what the high school runner might run.

Example: high school weekly training schedule

Sun.	Mon.	Tues.	Wed.	Thurs.	Fri.	Sat.
Easy	Speed work	Easy	Meet	Easy	Easy	Meet

In this weekly schedule, the high school runner has a track workout on Monday, easy run Tuesday, meet on Wednesday, and easy run on Thursday. Friday is an easy taper, with Saturday being a big Invitational meet with many schools attending. He then recovers on Sunday and repeats the pattern the next week.

Where are the hills? Where is the long run? Remembering the puzzle pattern, the Wednesday meet takes the place of the long run. After this meet, the high school runner can add some extra miles to his cool down to "count" as the long run.

The concept to remember is that the three hard days can be switched out for meets during the cross country season. When a meet does not fall on one of these days, treat this day as if it were a training day, running either a speed session, hill workout, or a long run.

This is a tough schedule, but the season is short and you have trained for this. Be smart. Run easy on your easy days, hard on your hard days, and really hard in your meets.

Example: middle school weekly training schedule

Sun.	Mon.	Tues.	Wed.	Thurs.	Fri.	Sat.
Easy	Easy	Speed work	Easy	Hills	Easy	Meet

In this example, the middle school runner has meets on Tuesdays and Saturdays. When there is not a Tuesday meet scheduled, the middle school runner will do a track session. Thursday is for hill workouts that will help the runner be strong in his races. When there is not a meet scheduled for Saturday, the runner can use this day for a long run.

Find the balance between challenging yourself and pushing too hard in your workouts. Save the heroics for race day.

💡 It is important NOT to push yourself to the point of throwing up. Running to the point of throwing up can lead to the same negative complications that bulimia creates, such as inflammation of the throat, tears of the esophagus, and dental cavities (Knowlton, 2011).

💡 Running should be fun! It should be about getting yourself into the best possible shape you can and being able to enjoy it your whole life long.

 Chapter 7

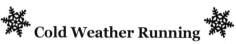 **Cold Weather Running**

Early one morning, I drove my car to meet several of my running friends for a very long run. Our plan was to drive to the Blue Ridge Parkway and run the "dark side of the mountain" on the trails. As I waited in the parking lot, the rain began to turn to sleet. Driving up to the trailhead, we began climbing and as we began climbing the rain mixed with sleet began to turn to snow. Soon the snow began to stick and accumulate. By the time we turned onto the Parkway, there was 4 inches of snow on the railings along the roadside.

We continued on, trying to figure out how we were going to get this run in. Since we had more runners coming from the other direction, we drove on to the Apple Orchard Falls wayside to meet them. The winding road along the parkway makes for a beautiful drive in good weather. But that day it became treacherous, as one of my friend's car began sliding sideways. We eventually made it to the meeting place to find snow 6 inches deep. What were we to do?

Wisely, one of us remembered that the Parkway closes in bad weather and he suggested that we get off the Parkway or risk being stuck there with the roads blocked off. We also decided to leave my friend's car there and have her ride with me in my 4-wheel drive vehicle.

Back in town, the weather wasn't as bad, just sleeting. We drove to the bike path to run the trails there in order to complete our long run. After one 6 mile loop, we were back at the cars. Only one other runner and I were willing to continue on in the harsh conditions, so we said goodbye to the others and headed back out.

I am not sure if it was from the sleet or my fatigue, but after only a few more miles I suddenly found myself falling through the air and knew that this was going to hurt. I landed hard on my knee and hands and splat into an icy puddle. I sat there for a few minutes trying to assess how badly I was injured. My knees and ankles all felt sore, but nothing was broken. I was just wet and my hands were cold and wet from landing in the puddle. My friend and I continued running, but decided to turn back after another mile.

When we eventually got back to our cars, I found that my hands were so numb that I could not turn the key to unlock my car. I was so glad that my friend was with me. She was able to unlock my car for me and waited until I started it and she knew I was on my way home. It took me quite some time to thaw out from that run.

Tips for running in cold weather

1. Be sure to dress in layers that can be shed as you warm up.
2. In very cold or windy weather, apply a thin layer of Vaseline to your face to protect yourself from windburn.
3. When running outside in snow or ice, adjust your pace to be more cautious and allow yourself more time as you watch out for black ice, which looks like wet pavement.
4. Be sure to wear a hat or headband when the temperatures drop, because you lose body heat through your head.
5. Hand warmers can be tucked into your gloves or pockets to keep your fingers from getting too cold.

 Chapter 8

Nitrition

Exercisers who eat before they work out have more energy and burn more fat.

Every year the cross country team would have a cookout at my house before the season began. Each family would bring their favorite summer dish and my husband would grill hotdogs and hamburgers for everyone. This was a fun time and often I was asked, "What should I eat before practice?" "What is a good post-run meal?"

It is important for everyone to eat a well balanced diet. It is even more important for the young runner, who is still growing, to eat enough of the right foods. Finding the right combination of which foods can be a bit tricky.

I recommend the young and beginning runner eat a ratio of 60-20-20 percent of carbohydrates, proteins, and fats daily. I use this easy-to-remember ratio from researchers who give a wider range for each basic food group (Mayo Clinic, 2011). Most items at a grocery store will have these amounts listed on the side of the package.

Runners can check to be sure they are getting enough of each food group.

When you run, bike, swim or play, your body incurs tiny tears in the muscles. This is normal. To help your body rebuild these muscles, it is important to consume 100-200 calories of a mix of carbohydrates and proteins after each workout.

One of the best post-workout foods is chocolate milk (Ivy, 2011). A glass of low-fat chocolate milk contains the proteins needed to rebuild your muscles along with the carbohydrates needed to begin refueling your energy supply. And it tastes good, too. You can follow that quick post workout drink with a well-rounded meal later.

While it is important to be sure to get enough protein in your diet, it can be easy to consume too much due to the popularity of protein drinks and energy bars. Be sure to read the labels and stay in the 20% daily range for both proteins and fats. This may sound like too high a percentage of fats, but fats are an important component to your diet. If you focus on your protein and carbohydrate amounts, you should get enough fat in your diet as well. Some people will cut all of the fat out of their diet, especially if they are trying to lose weight, but it is better to remember "all things in moderation." Your body needs fat just like it needs other nutrients, so keep this ratio in mind when choosing your foods.

One of my cross country runners shared her recipe for fruit smoothies with me. She loved to make these all summer long. What a great way to mix protein and carbohydrates in a tasty refreshing drink. Here is her recipe.

Fruit smoothies
½ cup vanilla yogurt (regular or low-fat)
1 banana
2 cups frozen strawberries (slightly thawed)
1 cups frozen blue berries (slightly thawed)
1 medium cored apple (with skin on)
Blend until smooth.
Makes 2 large servings.
225 calories per serving.

We all have busy schedules, so it is important to look at your day and find time to eat and know what to eat when you have a workout or a meet later in the day. Here are some guidelines I hope will help you when planning your meal or snack prior to a run.

 What to eat and when

1. If you have just 15 minutes before practice, have a little something rich in carbohydrates. Choose a small piece of fresh fruit, a sports drink, or a few pretzels.
2. If you have thirty to ninety minutes before exercise, have a snack of easily digestible carbohydrates and little or no protein such as a small banana with 1 tbsp. peanut butter, a glass of orange juice with toast, or 1 cup non-fat yogurt.
3. If you have two hours before a work out, eat a smaller meal that is light in protein and fat.
4. If your workout is four hours away, eat a regular meal that combines protein, fat and carbohydrates. (See meal suggestions below.)

💡 Finding what works best for you takes trial and error. Experiment with different foods while training, to be sure they don't upset your stomach.

I am often asked what a good post-workout meal would be. Here are a couple sample meals.

Breakfast
1 cup low-fat or non-fat flavored yogurt
1-2 slices toast with peanut butter
Sliced fresh strawberries or banana (optional)
1 glass orange juice

Lunch
1 cup chicken salad
2 slices whole wheat bread
1-2 slices tomato and lettuce
Glass of 2% milk
Pretzels
1 raw apple

Dinner
6 oz. grilled chicken or 4 oz. grilled steak
1-2 cups of pasta with tomato sauce
1-2 cups of green vegetables (either fresh or steamed)
1 cup of fruit
Water, tea, or other non-sugared drink

Each summer I liked to take my cross country team on a breakfast run across one of the Blue Ridge Mountains. We'd meet early in the morning and carpool up to the campground and picnic area located at the base of Flat Top Mountain in Virginia. Once everyone arrived, I gathered the runners and divided them up into two groups. One group would run the 4 miles across the mountain and the other group the flatter, 1 mile loop around the lake at the base. Those runners going over the mountain were then carpooled to the trailhead on the other side of the mountain and dropped off. From there, we ran the trail up to the top and stopped to let everyone catch up and for a photo-op. Then we continued down the other side of the mountain finishing at the picnic area where everyone had initially started. All the parents brought some breakfast food to compliment the pancakes my husband and I would grill.

Coach's famous pancake recipe

1 cup each: wheat four, white flour, and rolled oats
¼ cup olive oil
1 heaping tbsp. baking powder
1 egg
Milk – add until the desired consistency is reached
Mix all together and pour onto hot griddle. Flip when small bubbles appear in batter.
Makes 16-20 pancakes.

Being well hydrated means drinking enough water or other fluids throughout the day to keep your body in balance with the amount of water you lose through sweating and normal activity.

💡 It is good to drink a full glass of water as soon as you wake up.

How much should you drink? The common advice says for adults to drink eight-8oz. glasses of water or other liquids each day. When you add in the demands that puberty places on the body, plus the requirements of physical training, the result is that the young runner will need to consume at least this much fluid per day.

For a more accurate amount of how much fluid to drink, you can weigh yourself before you run and then again afterward. You should be drinking 16 ounces of fluid for every pound you lose through sweat during your run.

Another approach may be a little embarrassing, but it is to check the color of your urine. If it is clear or pale in color and odorless, then you are getting enough water in your diet (Mayo Clinic, 2011).

Know yourself and your fluid needs and be sure to adjust for the weather. You will need to drink more in hot weather, but when the weather turns cool you still need to drink enough liquids. Drinks such as juices, milk, and sports drinks, in addition to water, all count towards your hydration needs. Sports drinks contain the water you need plus carbohydrates sugar and a small amount of sodium and are good for before and after workouts, but add unnecessary calories if you drink them all the time. The perfect fluid is water, so be sure to drink plenty of water.

 Nutrition- recap

1. Eat a very light, carbohydrate-rich snack before an early morning run.

2. Be sure to eat something with both carbohydrates and protein after your run.

3. Choose healthy snacks while training and getting into shape. Fresh fruits and water are healthy alternatives to chips, cookies, and sodas.

Hydration- recap

1. Drink a large cup of water first thing in the morning every day.

2. Slow down. Don't push it in the heat.

3. If you start to feel chilled or upset to your stomach, it can mean that you are dehydrated. Stop running and drink some water or sports drink.

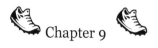 Chapter 9

Stretching

Saturday morning runs began to be the norm for me. They were a great way to get my long run in while catching up with my friends' lives. It was also a great way to pool the wealth of knowledge from my friends on any number of topics.

One such Saturday, I was having some pain along the outside of my leg and traveling from my hip down to my knee. As I was describing this to my buddies and trying to stretch at our water stop, one of my friends told me it was my iliotibial (IT) band. He then proceeded to show me this "great stretch" where he held onto the fence post, crossed one leg over the other and stuck his rear end out as he sat back into an imaginary chair. This looked very ridiculous and I was hesitant to try it in front of the whole group, but my pain insisted that I try something. To my surprise, as I sat into my "chair," the exact source of pain began to be stretched and felt a little better.

Another friend told me how she had had the same IT band problem and said that she would sit in an ice bath after each of her runs in order to "ice" the whole area of her legs. This also seemed pretty extreme, but I was willing to try different things and my friends seemed very sure of their advice.

After I finished that run and had done my regular stretching and my new "chair" stretch, I filled the bathtub with cold water, gritted my teeth and submerged my legs. After the initial shock of cold water subsided, I dumped the bucket of ice I had been instructed to add into the tub and waited. Fortunately for me, I had a cup of hot coffee and the newspaper to help me deal with the temperature dropping so suddenly and the fact that I was supposed to stay in there for ten minutes. So, I sipped and read and made it through my first ice bath and realized how GREAT my legs felt afterward. I decided that I would indeed do this again! I discovered that in the summertime, using an outdoor water hose on my legs right after a run helps, too.

One of the best investments you can make to avoid injury is spending time stretching your muscles. You don't have to spend a lot of time stretching; often just ten minutes after each run is all you need to keep your legs limber and injury free. The most effective stretching is done when your muscles are warm, for example, after a warm up walk or jog, or a warm shower.

💡 Be careful not to stretch immediately before a run, because your muscles are cold and more likely to tear (Harriman, 2012). Rather, stretch after a warm-up or at the end of your run as part of your cool down.

I recommend stretching these four main muscle groups: calves, quadriceps, hamstrings, and the muscles that support the hips. These can be easy to remember with these alliterative pairs: calves, quads and hamstrings, hips. You want to hold each stretch for 15-30 seconds (ACSM, 2010).

Here is the proper way to perform each stretch.

Calves Lean your hands against a wall, arms straight out in front of you, and position your back foot with the toes pointed slightly inward. Keep your back leg straight and heel down. Lean your torso towards the wall, bending your arms slightly, until you feel the stretch behind the knee and on your calf. Hold for a count of 15-30 seconds. Repeat with other leg. For a deeper calf stretch, start in the position described above and bend your back knee as you move your hips back over your foot. You should feel this deep in the calf. Hold for 15-30 seconds. Repeat on other side.

Quadriceps (Quads) Grab the shoelaces of one foot and pull that foot up behind you while balancing on the other foot. Keep your knees together and torso upright. For more of a stretch, flex the foot in your hand. Hold for 15-30 seconds. Repeat with other leg.

Hamstrings Flex one foot and place its heel either on the ground or on a chair, no higher than a 45 degree angle. Face the flexed leg and lean over to bring your chest towards your thigh. Hold for 15-30 seconds. Repeat with your other leg.

Hips Hold on to something and cross one leg over the other, with your ankle near the knee of the opposite, supporting leg. Sit back into an imaginary chair, keeping the supporting knee over the shoelaces of your foot. You should feel this in the hip of the bent leg. Hold for 15-30 seconds. Repeat on other side.

In addition to stretching after each run, it is good to strengthen your upper body and core. It is easy to lose good form at the end of a run when you are tired. If you have a strong core and arms you will be able to maintain good form all the way through your workout and races.

A few simple core exercises that I have found easy to add at the end of a workout are push-ups, planks, and crunches. Push-ups will help you develop strong arms needed to pump as you are sprinting those last few meters of a race. Planks help strengthen your back and core. Crunches will build strong abs that will help your posture remain upright with chest open and lungs free to fill up completely, while you focus on using your legs. The combination of these exercises will keep you from slouching when you get tired during a run, which inhibits lung capacity. Here is the proper way to perform each.

Push-ups Lie flat on the ground on your stomach. Put your hands under your shoulders and your feet flexed and positioned up on the toes. Push up, keeping your body straight from your shoulders to your heels until your arms are straight. Slowly lower your body by bending your arms, until your arms are at a right angle at the elbow and push back up. Repeat as many times as you can with good form.

Planks Lie on your stomach in the push-up starting position. Lift up your torso and position your elbows on the floor or mat directly under your shoulders with your hands out in front of you. Keeping your elbows and forearms on the floor or mat, contract your core and raise your body into a plank position, which is straight from shoulders to heels, and hold as long as you can. Rest and repeat one or two more times.

Crunches Lie on your back with your knees bent. With your feet about 12 inches from your bottom, put your hands behind your head with your elbows wide. Place an imaginary apple under your chin to keep your head in the correct position and contract your abs so that your shoulder blades lift off the ground. Pause briefly and lower. Be sure to keep your elbows wide and your chin away from your chest as you raise your shoulders upward. Repeat this for as many as you can with good form.

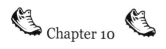 Chapter 10

All in a Day

One year after graduating and moving back to Central Virginia, we had our first child. Having children can definitely change your life and your priorities. Thankfully, I also had a very supportive husband who helped me carve out time in my busy day to still get in my runs. I want to mention that it was around this time that both my mother and mother-in-law played a very big role in my running. At this time my mother gave me a running journal to track my daily runs and my mother-in-law gave me my first sports watch, both of which have been key in my running career. I have faithfully written in my running journal for over thirty years, chronicling everything that has happened during my runs, from the weather to the tenth of a mile that I covered as well as what I did on my days off. Anyone who knows me knows that I am also addicted to my watch and to times, not only my own times, but I remember the times of almost every other person I've competed against.

Now, as a coach, I chart the progress of each of my runners and compare them to previous times and courses. I later learned not to be so strict about wearing a watch for every single run, but I still like reading not only my times but all my friends' and athletes' times, determining how they compare to previous years. I like to ponder where it may take them in the future. So, a big thanks to my moms!

After my second child, another daughter, was born, I told my husband that I wanted to see what would happen if I did that training I spoke of earlier. He said he would help in any way that he could. (What a guy!) And so began the evenings when he would come home from work and I would run and make my trips to the local track for speed work. The following year was what I like to call my "PR year" because almost every time I laced up my shoes and toed the starting line, I ran a Personal Record or PR. Consistently running faster than the last time you ran is not an easy thing to do. God was blessing my hard work and training.

During that time, I was also becoming more involved with our local running club and I signed up for the summer race series. This was a big motivator for me and I found that I raced more often than I would have had I not wanted to win that final award. Each race found me chasing one other woman for the top spot. She pushed me to work hard and helped my times continually creep down. With the final race of the series being the Virginia 10 Miler, I knew she would win the overall series award. As I said earlier, the 10 Miler is a very large race. Therefore, it wasn't until later that I learned she had not run in it. This opened the door for me and I won the Women's Overall series plaque for that year. I was on a roll. Nothing could stop me now!

Ever feel like that? Well, life and reality have a way of interfering with our dreams. Soon we were moving again so my husband could go back to college. A year after that we moved another time, bought a house, and welcomed child number three, a son. Two years after that, child number four, a second son, came into our home. I would not trade my family for the world, but somewhere in the back of my mind was that unfinished business with running. I needed to make it work.

Not wanting to sacrifice anything, I started getting up very early in the morning to run and be home before my family was awake. This worked extremely well, allowing me the time to devote to my family as well as my training. When I was getting up at 4:45 a.m., it was very important that I went to bed early enough to ensure I still got enough sleep. This was tough, but doable and well worth it.

When my children were old enough to run, they came with me to the track while I did workouts and also to races. Sometimes they ran in a race themselves, if there was a shorter distance offered.

Our local running club had a summer track series in June that offered 100 meter runs each week along with the main event, a longer distance race. My children competed in these 100 meter runs and when they got old enough, they ran in the main events. When they were ready to compete on a cross country team, there was nothing available to them as homeschool students. Being the fixer that I am and seeing the need, I began the process that led to creating the first homeschool cross country team in the nation: The Peaks View Pacers.

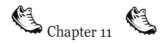 Chapter 11

The Race

The training is done.
Now, BELIEVE in yourself!

Foot Locker South Regional Cross Country
Championships in Charlotte, NC, is the end of the
season race for many runners, including me. One
year, it had been very rainy the week leading up to
it. I wanted to walk the course the night before in
case there were some flooded areas. Most of the
course was fine, but there was one section that had
a puddle that resembled a small pond. In walking
this, I observed that the sides were extremely
muddy and I mentally planned to run straight
through the middle of the puddle, thinking that if I
tried to go around it, I might lose my shoe in the
deep mud.

The next morning was the race and as I ran this
section I went right down the middle, just as
planned, knowing I was sacrificing my nice white
shoes to the puddle but focusing only on the race.
When the race was over and I was catching my
breath, I looked down to see that not a single drop
of mud or water had clung to my shoes. I knew I
had been running fast and figured this must have

been the reason; my foot went into the water and then out again so quickly that there was not enough time for the water to move back into my shoe. I had stumbled onto a race strategy that I might not have thought of otherwise. That year, I won the Women's Master's Division.

💡 If you have a puddle or a creek to cross, keep running straight through it. If you slow down to figure things out, you are more likely to get your shoes wet.

💡 It is a good idea to walk the course of each cross country meet before the race. This helps you become familiar with the terrain and various obstacles you may encounter.

The things you do before a race are just as important as the actual race itself. I have already discussed the training aspect of race preparation. Now I want to look at the mental and practical side of getting ready for a race.

I have heard it said that a race is 85% mental. What that means is that whatever you mentally think about yourself and the race will influence your physical ability to perform in the race. If you think negatively, even though you have properly trained, chances are you will have a poor performance. On the other hand, if you believe in yourself and your training and your ability to run the race well, you will often outperform your expectations.

In order to prepare mentally, you need to "see" yourself running the race and finishing strong. As your race approaches, begin going through the course in your mind. At each obstacle, picture yourself going smoothly over the jump, through the creek, passing the runners and then completing the course comfortably and strong. This will give you confidence and help you when you are in the actual race.

I have found it good to have three goals going into a race. The first goal is one that you are certain you can achieve with a minimum amount of effort. The second goal is one you think you can achieve if you try. And the third goal is the one that you can achieve if the weather is perfect, you are well-rested and injury-free, and the heavens open up and God looks down on you and smiles.

Having these three goals prepares you to feel good about yourself at the end of the race, regardless of the outcome. Sometimes runners set too high a goal for themselves, one that is unrealistic. They are then disappointed when they do not reach that goal. You should never leave a race feeling bad about yourself. If you have done your homework and trained well you should be proud of your accomplishment, whichever goal you ultimately achieve. So be sure not to set the bar too high when setting your race goals, and follow my three-step goal setting pattern to help you be proud of your race accomplishment.

The day before your race, be sure to drink plenty of water and eat carbohydrate-rich foods. A pasta meal the night before your meet is an excellent way to help your body store up the energy it needs to get you through your race. A 5k race is not super long, so there is no need to eat extra carbohydrates.

Coach Jones' favorite pre-race meal
    1-2 cups cooked spaghetti
    1 cup tomato sauce
    1-2 cups green leaf tossed salad
    Low-fat Italian dressing
    1 slice bread with light butter
    Parmesan cheese to top
    Water to drink

The night before your race, plan ahead and lay out the clothes and shoes that you plan to wear in the race. That way you will not be scrambling around looking for your uniform at the last minute.

Check the weather for the next day to see what you will need to wear. If the race day weather is cold, you will want to dress in layers. Unless the weather is extremely cold, you will still race in your singlet and shorts with maybe some gloves or a hat for extra warmth. If the race is very cold, layer a long-sleeved moisture wicking shirt underneath your uniform. Otherwise, plan to layer long sleeves and pants over your uniform. Layers will help you stay warm all through your warm-up and stretches; you can take them off just before the start.

Running when you feel a little cold is better than running too hot; keep that in mind as you plan your race clothes. If you have your race number and safety pins, go ahead and pin them on the front of your uniform top or racing shirt. Do as much as you can the night before. This takes the stress and jitters off the next morning, when you should be visualizing your fast finish.

NOTHING NEW ON RACE DAY!!
Whatever you eat or drink, be sure to have tried it during training.

The morning of a race, you will want to drink a large glass of water immediately after you wake up. If your race is later in the day, you want to drink water all day long, stopping about 1-2 hours before your race. Eat your normal prerace meal 2 hours or more before your race. You need 2 hours to digest, so eat whatever you have been having before practices. You can have a sip or two of water just before the race. Some Gatorade or an energy bar 15 minutes before the start is okay, too, but only if you have practiced eating or drinking it in training.

At the race site, be mindful of your need to use the bathroom. Be sure to take care of that need early on so you are not looking for a bathroom as they are calling you to the start line. Plan ahead. Warm up with a light jog for about 5-15 minutes. Keep your warm-up clothes on until the very last minute. Feeling a little cooler as the race begins will help you have a faster start. Do some light stretching and have one last sip of water. Continue going over the course in your mind.

Concentrate on the positives. If the weather is hot, think about the cool breeze. If it is rainy, be thankful the sun is not glaring down. Take any and all negatives and turn them into positives. Stay relaxed and ready.

On the starting line, be sure to double knot your shoelaces to avoid them coming untied during the race.

When the gun goes off at the start, you want to go out quickly. You should start a little faster than your goal pace and put yourself in a good position. Because it will be a shorter distance than most of your training runs, you can run faster. If you have runners in front of you, focus on one at a time as you catch them and pass them confidently. If you are out front, don't listen for them to catch you. Concentrate on your form; stay relaxed and keep your arms pumping strong. Focus on the course and your position amongst the other runners. Make sure that your stride is fluid and that you are moving smoothly as you continue to move forward.

Keep the frequency of your footfalls high by picking your feet up and putting them down quickly. I call this the Four F's of racing: focus, form, fluid, and frequency. Periodically do a body-check to make sure these are all in sync. This will help you get to the finish line in good form and help you achieve your goal time.

Many training books will tell you to start off slowly in a race. Often these books are speaking to adults who are training for a half-marathon or a marathon. In shorter races, you want to go out a little faster than race pace. The following excerpt is from research on collegiate runners, so the young runner will want to adjust the exact times when figuring out how much faster his first mile should be.

> "Researchers from the University of New Hampshire examined the effect of different pacing strategies on 5-K performance. Their subjects were 11 female runners from the school's cross-country team, who trained an average of 35 miles per week and had 5-K PRs ranging from 18 to 21 minutes. After running two 5-K time trials to establish a baseline pace, the subjects then completed three more 5-Ks using decidedly different pacing strategies: The subjects ran the first mile of each race either equal to, three

percent faster, or six percent faster than their established baseline pace per mile. After the first mile, the subjects could change their pace to finish as quickly as possible.

The results surprised everyone familiar with the go-out-easy approach. Eight of the 11 women ran their best 5-K times (averaging 20:39) when they ran the first mile six percent faster than their baseline pace. The other three subjects posted their best times (20:52) going out three percent faster than baseline pace. The even-paced runners produced the slowest times, averaging 21:11. The faster-starting women did slow down more during the race, but the even-paced runners simply couldn't make up the time lost in a slower start.

So how is it that these runners achieved their best times by logging their first mile a seemingly suicidal 26 seconds faster than their predicted 5-K pace? According to the study, at the end of the first mile, the even-paced runners were at only 78 percent of their VO2 max, an effort level more akin to a tempo run than a 5-K race--below their potential. The three-percent and six-percent faster starts put the subjects at 82 and 83 percent of VO2 max after the first mile, which is closer to the intensity you'd expect from an experienced runner racing the first mile of a 5-K.

So should we all go out as fast as possible in every race? Not exactly. Moderately trained runners may benefit from a faster start because they're probably not starting fast enough in the first place...." (Runner's World, 2007).

Remember the Four F's of racing:

1. **Focus** – on the race and your position
2. **Form** – your arms are relaxed and pumping
3. **Fluid** –your strides are fluid and smooth
4. **Frequency** – the cadence of your pace is high

In the middle of a race or training run, do a body check. Ask yourself, "How are my legs feeling?" "What does my breathing sound like?" "Am I relaxed?" Take some time to shake out your arms and maybe roll your shoulders back. Then ask, "How much further do I need to run?" and, "Do I think I can pick it up here?"

After your race, try not to collapse at the finish line. Keep moving. Walk around until your breathing and heart rate return to normal and then get some water or sports drink. Gather your teammates and go for an easy jog and then stretch. If you need or want to, you can jog for longer, to get in the long run miles; the race is over. Sometimes it is good to find the winner of the race and ask if he wants to jog with you. Then, ask him about the race. You might pick up some tips. After your cool down, be sure to get some food. A little protein with your carbohydrates will help repair any muscle damage.

Remember to stretch well after you have finished running. It is easy to forget, but stretching after your race will help you recover and not be so sore the next day. Take a few minutes and stretch. When you stretch, you want to stretch the four main muscle groups: calves, quads, hamstrings, and hips. (See stretching above for the proper form of each.) And keep drinking fluids for the rest of the day.

Recap:

- Nothing new on race day.

- Walk the course beforehand.

- Set out race clothes the night before.

- Be positive and visualize a strong performance.

- Start fast.

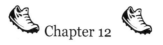 Chapter 12

This and That

What to wear when running

Synthetic fibers, such as Coolmax, Dryleet, Spandex, etc., are good fabrics that wick sweat away from the body and dry quickly. I recommend wearing a tank top, or singlet, and shorts made from one of these fabrics. Cotton is not a good fabric to wear when running because it absorbs sweat, becomes heavy, and can cause chaffing. If you plan to run when the weather is cooler, add a long-sleeved top and long pants to your wardrobe. Gloves and a hat can also help keep you warm on those colder runs. The important thing to remember is the fabric; avoid cotton for your runs.

Shoes

It is also important to choose the right shoes. If your town doesn't have a running store where you can go in and be fitted by a shoe specialist, remember these tips for choosing your shoes. Shoes should be flexible in the toe box and very lightweight. Avoid shoes that are heavy and stiff. New Balance, Saucony, Asics, Brooks, and Nike are just a few name brands that offer good quality shoes. Shoes also need to be replaced regularly. As you run in your shoes, you begin to break down the insole and support system of the shoe. Once that is broken down, it can no longer support your foot in the way in which it was designed. If you start to experience foot, knee or hip pain, it often can be traced back to your shoes. Most shoes last for about 250-350 miles, so be sure to keep a running log to help you track how many miles you have on your shoes. I have two pairs of shoes that I alternate for my runs. This allows for the cushioning in them to spring back to its original form in between runs. That way, I always have a fresh, dry pair when I go on my run.

If your shoes should get wet from running in the rain or a creek crossing, stuff them tightly with paper towels. Remove the towels the next day and they should be almost completely dry. Then, leave them to air dry the rest of that day.

Keeping track of how many miles are on each shoe can be tricky, so here is what I do. I write a letter on the back of each pair of shoes, "A" and "B", or another letter or symbol, to let me know which pair is which. Then I write how many miles were run on each shoe each day in my running log.

Running Log

A running log is a journal where you write down the distance, location, and conditions for each of your runs. Keeping a journal can help you in many different ways. You can track your progress and see how many miles you run each day and the total miles for each week. This helps you increase your miles safely.

A running log allows you to look back to see what type of training worked for which workout or race. This is a very valuable tool when trying to recapture that "peak" performance. It also helps you keep track of how many miles you have run on your shoes; too many miles on one pair of shoes can result in injury. Any pain, or overall ache, in your hips, knees, or legs may mean it is time to change your shoes.

How to get around other runners in a race

I think it is important to show good sportsmanship during a race, but it is also important to protect yourself and be able to run your best. Many times the cross country course will narrow down to a single lane and it is important to know how to protect your position as well as pass when you come upon a slower runner. Passing on the left is the common running protocol, but politely saying, "passing on the left" may not always alert the runner ahead of you that you plan to pass so they can move over. Therefore, it is good to know how to pass effectively.

As you attempt to pass, remember to keep your elbows out a little so that you are not knocked off balance, if you should come into physical contact with the other runner. You also want to be decisive when you pass. Don't hesitate halfway through your pass. Speed up and hold that speed all the way around the runner. You want to give him the impression that you are in control and not to be challenged, so be sure to look strong, relaxed, and confident as you pass.

> Your goal is to feel "well within yourself" and as though you are running "on top of the ball," springing forward and very light.

On top of the ball
This is a phrase I use to describe the feeling I want you to experience when you are running. As you run, imagine yourself running on top of a ball, with your feet landing directly underneath you and your shoulders and hands relaxed. You feel light and your running is well within yourself, even when pushing up hills or doing intervals on the track. The opposite feeling is like you are running up the backside of the ball. This feeling is heavy and always striving. A slight adjustment in your form moves your upper torso and arms into a more forward position and the top of the ball feeling is achieved.

No boxing

Imagine your arms and legs as parts of the wheels of a train, moving forward and up and down in a smooth motion. The swinging motion your arms produce will want to be in this line. When a runner tires, it is easy for his arms to take on the look of a boxer, crossing in front of his body as he swings, rather than staying in the forward motion. Therefore, avoid boxing while running.

Runner's high

I recently started training a beginning runner for his first marathon. He had run a half-marathon with only a few miles of training during each of the weeks leading up to the race. He then came to me for a more structured plan. He wanted to do some sort of exercise most days of the week and run four days a week. After just a couple weeks on our new plan, he confided in me that he was feeling so fit and jazzed and thought he may have even lost a few pounds. He then confessed that he had considered running his whole week's worth of miles in one day to "get caught up." I could tell he was experiencing what is called a "runner's high." Runner's high is defined as "a feeling of euphoria that is experienced by some individuals engaged in strenuous running and that is held to be associated with a release of endorphins by the brain" according to the Merriam Webster dictionary. It is this runner's high that can lead to overtraining. When you feel so good and fit and able to do anything that you might consider running more miles that you should. Be aware of this. This is why you sit down and plan your training ahead of time, without feelings or emotions to guide your choices.

After the cross country season

Take a break. Now is a great time to recover from the summer and fall of hard training. Take some time off completely. Run only when you want and only what you want. If you feel tired and don't want to run, don't. This is a time to rest. Your break should last up to three months.

If you are planning on some post-season races, take a week off after your last regular season race, first. Then, you can continue with your training, running speed and hill workouts, until your late fall race(s) have been run. Following the post-season races, be sure you take some time off completely to recover.

Studies have shown that you can take as many as two weeks off without losing your fitness (Quinn, 2012). Listen to your body and take a day or two off each week to help your body recover from your workouts.

When to start back

In late February or early March you should begin your base training. Follow the weekly training plan mentioned earlier in this book. This is when you want to pull your calendar out and mark those key meets and races. Do not time yourself on these runs.

💡 Enjoy running. If you are not, maybe you need to do something different to make it fun. Join a training group. Run your normal route in the opposite direction. Put your arms out like you're flying on every downhill. Leave your watch at home. Enjoy yourself!

Finding ways to make your running more fun doesn't need to be difficult. One year my sister and I were running the Disney Marathon. It was her first marathon and we were running it together. We each wore matching shirts with our names on the front and "Big Sis" and "L'il Sis" written on the back. We skipped through Cinderella's Castle, which made everyone around us smile. Throughout the race we stopped and had our pictures taken with several of the Disney characters. Going through Epcot Center, with less than 5 miles to go, we skipped again going over the bridge, just because it seemed like a good idea. We had so much fun. As we were running the final stretch to the finish line, we pulled out a banner that read "Sisters go the distance" and we each held on to an end as we crossed the finish line. Each of these things helped to make the race fun and memorable. Plan ways to make your runs more fun, too.

Just for laughs

What Happens if Your Mom is a Runner...

- You were weaned on Gatorade
- You drink from cups won at races
- Your first shoes were Nike
- You learned math by helping your mom figure out her splits for the distance she just ran
- You learned to run almost before you could talk
- You are the most flexible kid in your neighborhood
- Your sandbox is the long jump pit when your mother runs track
- You find it difficult to understand that not everybody speaks runner lingo: PR, 5K, Splits, intervals, etc.
- On Saturday mornings you watch all the adventure races and track meets that had been taped that week instead of cartoons
- If you happen to see some safety pins lying around, you automatically put them in groups of four
- You learn to take off long-sleeved shirts for the short-sleeved shirt underneath, while running, before you turned nine
- You compare roller coasters with running 100 meter sprints
- You go shopping at the race expo

- You quickly learn that running is contagious
- Almost everybody in your city is acquainted with you because they run with your mother
- You don't have a dog because they are "runner eaters"

Written by my daughter, Beth Jones, at age 10, who adds, "These are things that really happened to my siblings and me."

Appendix A

Sample Training Plans
(Sample plans and workouts may be copied without written permission.)
Level One Training

A sample schedule would look like this:

	Sun	Mon	Tu	Wed	Th	Fri	Sat	Total
Wk 1	Rest	1	1	1	1	R	1	5
Wk 2	Rest	1	1	1	1	R	2	6
Wk 3	Rest	1	2	1	1	R	2	7
Wk 4	Rest	1	2	1	2	R	2	8
Wk 5	Rest	1	2	1	2	R	3	9
Wk 6	Rest	2	2	1	2	R	3	10
Wk 7	Rest	2	3	1	2	R	3	11
Wk 8	Rest	2	3	1.5	3	R	3	12.5
Wk 9	Rest	2	3	2	3	R	4	14
Wk 10	Rest	2	3	2	3	R	5	15
Wk 11	Rest	2	4	2	3.5	R	5	16.5
Wk 12	Rest	3	4	2	4	R	5	18

If you are a beginner, start by walk/jogging until you can complete a full mile without walking. Once you can run a mile every other day, you can try adding additional days. Then you are ready for the above training plan. If your schedule doesn't allow you to run every day, running every other day is fine. This is a guideline. The important thing is to not run two hard days back to back.

 For middle school runners

You may "level" off at any of these weeks once you reach week 6 and are running 10 miles per week. If your goal is to be in the top 5-7 on the team, I recommend running up to15 miles per week, using this as a guide. Be sure to listen to your body and back off if anything is hurting.

 For high school runners

Once you reach week 10, you may continue on to Level Two. I like high school runners to run 20-30 miles per week.

Level Two Training Schedule

For most high school runners

	Sun	Mon	Tu	Wed	Thu	Fri	Sat	Total
Wk 1	Rest	2	4	2	3.5	R	5	16.5
Wk 2	Rest	3	4	2	4	R	5	18
Wk 3	Rest	3	4	2	4	R	6	19
Wk 4	Rest	3	4	3	4	R	6	20
Wk 5	Rest	3	5	3	4	R	6	21
Wk 6	Rest	3	5	3	5	R	6	22
Wk 7	Rest	3	5	3	5	R	7	23
Wk 8	Rest	3	6	3	6	R	7	25
Wk 9	Rest	3	6	3	6	R	8	26
Wk 10	Rest	4	6	3	6	R	8	27
Wk 11	Rest	4	6	3	6	2	8	29
Wk 12	Rest	4	6	3	6	3	8	30

Weeks 4 and 10 are good weeks to "hold." If you feel tired or something starts to hurt, take a day or two off before resuming training. It is better to rest now, than risk getting injured later in the training plan.

Level Three Training Schedule

For the intermediate to advanced high school runner

	Sun	Mon	Tu	Wed	Thu	Fri	Sat	Total
Wk 1	Rest	3	5	3	5	R	7	23
Wk 2	Rest	3	6	3	6	R	7	25
Wk 3	Rest	3	6	3	6	R	8	26
Wk 4	Rest	4	6	3	6	R	8	27
Wk 5	Rest	4	6	3	6	2	8	29
Wk 6	Rest	4	6	3	6	3	8	30
Wk 7	Rest	4	6	4	6	3	9	32
Wk 8	Rest	4	7	4	7	3	9	34
Wk 9	Rest	4	8	4	7	3	9	35
Wk 10	Rest	4	8	4	8	3	9	36
Wk 11	Rest	5	8	4	8	4	9	38
Wk 12	Rest	5	8	5	8	4	10	40

Weeks 4, 6, and 10 are good weeks to "hold." If you feel tired or something starts to hurt, take a day or two off before resuming training. It is better to rest now, than risk getting injured later on in the training plan.

 Appendix B

Sample Workouts

Long run Add 1 mile to your longest run until you are running 5-10 miles for your long run, depending on your age and goals. A runner 13 and younger should not run farther than 5 miles for his longest run. He is still growing and should not impede that. Older runners may run up to 10 miles at one time, but should not run farther than 10 in a single training session.

Hill work Run a hill that takes you 30-60 seconds to climb. Push the hill by running fast and hard all the way to the top and then jog to the bottom. Repeat this 4-8 times, starting with 4 times and increasing 1 repeat each week until you are running 8 repeats. Cool down with a 1 mile or longer jog. (Note: A second hill with a different angle of elevation can be added for high school runners.)

Drills These include high-knees, butt-kicks, skipping, criss-cross sideways running, and strides. A description of each is given below. These can be done for 30 seconds out and 30 seconds back on your running path in the middle or at the end of a run.

- **High-Knees** Bring your knees up as high as you can as quickly as you can. Your steps will be short and quick. This builds the hamstring muscles while keeping a fast turnover.

- **Butt-Kicks** Lean forward slightly as you bring your feet back and up to your buttocks before kicking through the front part of your stride. This is also done quickly with small steps forward.

- **Skipping** Similar to when you skipped as a child, this type of skipping differs by having a more vertical focus. As you swing your opposite arm and knee forward, bring your knee up as high as you can before landing and bringing the next arm and knee forward and up.

- **Criss-Cross Sideways Running** Take a step to the right side with the right leg. With your left leg, cross over in front of the right leg moving toward the right. Take another step to the right with the right leg. This time, cross behind the right leg with the left leg. Continue stepping to the side and alternating crossing in front of the right leg and behind it all while moving to the right. Your arms will swing across your body in opposite timing to your legs. Once you have the form down, do this as quickly as you can while still maintaining good form and an upright posture. Repeat, going toward the left side and starting with the left leg.

- **Strides** Run a distance of 50-100 meters with the first third of your distance run gradually building speed and concentrating on form: shoulders relaxed, arms and knees forward, head up. The middle third of the distance is at your top speed, still focusing on form. The last third is a gradual reduction in speed. Strides are used to produce a quick turn over while using good form. Strides are always run at the end of a workout and at the beginning of a race.

Pick-ups These are designed to introduce your body to speed. In the middle of a run, after you have run at least one mile warm-up, begin picking up the pace for 30 seconds to 1 minute, with 30 seconds to 1 minute recovery. Each pick-up should be quick, but slower than your 5k race pace. The focus is more on your form than on your speed. Check that you are relaxed across your shoulders and that your arms are swinging front-to-back, not side-to-side and that you are picking up your legs like a sprinter. Remember the Four F's of racing? These are excellent to practice in training as well: Focus, Form, Fluid, and Frequency. You should feel strong and in control while running a faster than usual pace. Visualize yourself running "on top of the ball" as opposed to running "up the side of the ball." You can run up to 2 minutes fast with 2 minute recovery. Only run 10% of your weekly miles in total speed miles.

Tempo run After a mile warm-up, pick up your pace to a "comfortably hard" pace and hold for 1-2 miles (Luff, 2011). Comfortably hard should be fast, but not race pace. Continue running as you slow back down to your original easy pace for another mile. The tempo run is designed to increase your lactate threshold level and help you get comfortable with a faster pace run over a longer distance.

Speed work Run 1 mile warm-up. Then run 4-8 x 400 meters at a faster than your 1 mile race pace. Start with 4 repeats, and add one repeat each week until you reach 8 repeats. Cool down with a 1 mile jog. When doing these shorter distances on the track, challenge yourself to see how fast you can run, knowing you will have to do so many repeats. That is how you get faster—by running faster. (See Ladder sample below.)

Run your warm up and cool down in the reverse direction when running on the track. This keeps your legs from becoming too stressed on one side.

Speed work: LADDER Warm up with a 1 mile jog. On the track run each distance hard, then jog the recovery distance.

> 200 meters with 200 meters recovery
> 400 meters – w/ 400 meters recovery
> 800 meters – w/ 400 meters recovery
> 1200 meters – w/ 400 meters recovery
> 800 meters – w/ 400 meters recovery
> 400 meters – w/ 400 meters recovery
> 200 meter – w/ 200 meters recovery

(This example is for a runner doing 2.5 miles in speed)

Be sure to consult the 10% rule for the total miles of speed you can run. Run each repeat steady and quick. Make sure your heart rate and breathing return to the point where you can talk without gasping during the rest interval before you start the next repeat. If you need a little longer recovery, take it. Then, steadily come back down the ladder. Run each one at or below the previous time, finishing with a very quick 200 meters.

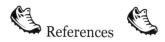 References

American College of Sports Medicine (2010). *ACSM's resources for the Personal Trainer, 3ʳᵈ ed.* Lippincott, Williams, & Wilkins. Baltimore, MD, and Philadelphia, PA.

Eyestone, E. (2007). Go out fast in your next 5K: To run your best 5-k, new research suggests a more aggressive approach. *Runner's World, March 26.* Retrieved from http://www.runnersworld.com/article/0,71 20,s6-238-244-259-11738-0,00.html

Fiore, K. (2010). To stay trim, women need an hour of exercise daily. *Medpage Today, March 21.* Retrieved from http://www.medpagetoday.com/PrimaryCa re/ExerciseFitness/19187

Harriman, D. (2012). Should you stretch cold muscles? *Livestrong.com, April 29.* Retrieved from http://www.livestrong.com/article/462832-should-stretch-cold-muscles/

Healthfinder (2012). Help your child stay at a healthy weight. Retrieved from http://healthfinder.gov/prevention/ViewTo picFull.aspx?topicID=62

Hind, K. and Burrows, M. (2007). Weight-bearing exercise and bone mineral accrual in children and adolescents: A review of controlled trials. *Bone, 40(1),* 14-27.

Ivy, J. (2011). Chocolate milk gives athletes leg-up after exercise, says University of Texas at Austin Study. *The University of Texas at Austin: News, June 22.* Retrieved from http://www.utexas.edu/news/2011/06/22/milk_studies

Knowlton, S. (2011). Bulimia side effects. *Health Guidance: Eating Disorders.* Retrieved from http://www.healthguidance.org/entry/15536/1/Bulimia-Side-Effects.html

Latter, P. (2011). Josh McDougal at a crossroads: The rise, fall and rebirth of Josh McDougal. *Running Times Magazine, April 23.* Retrieved from http://www.runnersworld.com/college-runner-profiles/josh-mcdougal-rossroads?page=single

Luff, C. (2011). Train to run your fastest 5k-intermediate training plan; How to improve your 5k time. *About.com.* Retrieved from http://running.about.com/od/racetraining/a/intermediate5K.htm

Luff, C. (2012). Lactate threshold. *About.com Running & Jogging, May 30*. Retrieved from http://running.about.com/od/trainingessentials/g/lactatethreshhold.htm

Lydiard, A. and Hashizume, N. (2004). Five circles; *Understanding the Lydiard method for the 21st Century. Prepared by Nozzy Hashizume, August.* Retrieved from http://lydiardfoundation.org/training/understandinglydiardmethod.aspx

Mayo Clinic staff (2011). Dehydration – definition. *Mayo Clinic Diseases and Conditions: Dehydration- Definition.* Retrieved from http://www.mayoclinic.com/health/dehydration/DS00561

Mayo Clinic staff (2011). Healthy diet: End the guesswork with these nutrition guidelines. *Mayo Clinic In-Depth, August 2.* Retrieved from http://www.mayoclinic.com/health/healthy-diet/NU00200

Quinn, E. (2012). How to maintain fitness during breaks and holidays. *About.com Sports Medicine.* Retrieved from http://sportsmedicine.about.com/od/strengthtraining/a/112105.htm

Road Runners Club of America Coaching
        Certification (2009). *Fundamentals of
        Coaching Science and Art.* Wy'East
        Consulting and Team Oregon, 2004-2009.

Made in the USA
Columbia, SC
04 May 2021